CONTENTS

MANAGERS

1.When was Brendan Rodgers Liverpool manager?

2.How many reigns did Kenny Dalglish have as Liverpool manager?

3.How many trophies did Rafa Benitez win as Liverpool Manager?

4.When was Graeme Souness manager Liverpool?

5.How many trophies did Bob Paisley win as Liverpool manger?

6.Who was the first Liverpool manager?

7.Who did Jurgen Klopp manage before Liverpool?

8.In 2010 Ex-liverpool manager Roy Hodgson said that Liverpool Fc weren't two big for what?

9.What is Jurgen Klopps middle name?

10.What three trophies did Houllier win in one season

MANAGERS

11. What other Premier league teams did Rafa Benitez manage?

12. What country was Bill Shankly born in?

13- What manager famously said "Fact!" in a pre match press conference rant?

14- How many managers have Liverpool had in the premier league era?

15- What type of music has Jurgen Klopp's playing style been compared to?

16- What Liverpool manager, then player couldn't make his playing debut due to serving in the army during WW2

17- Which Liverpool manager is a huge Bollywood fan?

18- Who took Bill Shankly's job upon his retirement?

19- What football team did Jurgen Klopp spend most of his career playing for?

20- Which Ex-Liverpool manager was made an inaugural inductee of the English football Hall of fame?

MANAGERS

21-Where did ex-Liverpool manager Brendan Rodgers start his playing career?

22-How many caps did Bill Shankly have for Scotland?

23-Which Ex-Liverpool managers brother is a country music artist?

24-Where did Bill Shankly start his managerial career?

25-How many Liverpool managers have won the champions league?

26-Who won Liverpool's first premier league?

27.Who was the first ever player-manager in English football?

28.Who is the clubs most successful manager having won 21 trophies?

29.What does Jurgen Klopp ban players from doing until they win a major trophy?

30. What item belonging to Liverpool manager Jurgen Klopp was famously broken in their 5-4 comeback win against Norwich in the 15/16 season?

MANAGERS

31. Who was it that broke said item in the previous question whilst celebrating?

32. Which Liverpool manager famously said Liverpool was made for me and I was made for Liverpool."?

33. Which Liverpool manager holds the record for biggest win?

34. Alternatively which Liverpool manager holds the record for their biggest defeat?

35 Between 1990 and 2001 which club did now Liverpool manager Jurgen Klopp make over 300 appearances for?

36. Which former Liverpool manager worked with Jose Mourinho as a youth coach while at Chelsea?

37. Which Liverpool manager won the club their first league title?

38. Liverpool are hoping to end their 16-year drought of the FA cup this season after advancing to the semi-finals, with which manager did they last win the prestigious trophy?

39. Now Liverpool manager Jurgen Klopp joined Liverpool in 2015, but what year did he win his first trophy with the reds?

40. Which Liverpool manager has had the longest reign in charge of the club?

MANAGERS

40. Which Liverpool manager has had the longest reign in charge of the club?

41. In 2017 which former Liverpool manager had a stand named after him

42. Which Liverpool manager is known for saying "Boom"?

43. In 2020 the documentary Three Kings was released, this featured Matt busby, Jock stein and which former Liverpool manager?

44. How many of Liverpool's former managers failed to win a trophy with the club?

45. Sir Kenny Dalglish is considered one of Liverpool's best players and most influential managers, but which former Liverpool manager signed him?

46. Who was the last person to manage Liverpool that also played for them?

47. Jurgen Klopp ended Liverpool's wait for a premier league trophy in the 19-20 season, but who was the last manager to win a league title with Liverpool before the German?

48. Which assistant manager did Jurgen Klopp famously fall out with at Liverpool?

49. Which former manager won a treble with Liverpool in 1984 making them the first treble winning team in England?

50. Which former Liverpool manager and player now regularly works for sky sports as a pundit on matches?

PLAYERS

1.Who is Liverpools all time record goal scorer?

2. Who is Liverpools all time record appearances?

3.Which two players have held the record for fastest premier league hat trick?

4.How did Danish goalkeeper Michael Stensgaard dislocate his shoulder shortly after joining the club?

5.Liverpool had the record for most expensive defender and goalkeeper before which other premier league club made a purchase in 2018/19?

6.Whats Mo Salah's actual name?

7.Which current Liverpool famously covered the "Allez Allez Allez" chant on guitar?

8.Which current Liverpool player joined Liverpool after playing for Groningen, Celtic and Southampton?

9.Which two Liverpool players competed against eachother in the 2021 AFCON final?

10.Which infamous Italian striker did Liverpool sign to replace Luiz Suarez?

PLAYERS

11.Which boyhood Liverpool fan joined the club from Southampton in the 14/15 season?

12.Which Ex-Liverpool player urinated on the goalpost as he believed the club was cursed by a witch doctor?

13-Which Liverpool player played seven times on New Years Day, scoring in all seven?

14-Who was the first player to score in two separate Fa Cup finals?

15-Who is the only Liverpool player to ever score a hat trick in three separate competitions in one season?

16-Who is the only Liverpool player to score three consecutive hat tricks for the reds?

17-What player scored a hat trick in six different competitions?

18-How many bookings did Ian Callaghan have in his 857 games for Liverpool?

19-How many players have made more than 200 appearances without scoring a goal?

20-Which current Liverpool player holds the record for goals in a premier league season?

PLAYERS

21- Which Liverpool player scored his only goal for the club in a league cup final- being the only player to score their only goal in a final?

22-Who scored the clubs quickest Champions league goal of all time?

23-Who was the last player to score on their birthday?

24-How many players have scored for Liverpool on every day of the week?

25- How many of those players currently play for Liverpool?

26-Who had to change their number from 25 to 12 to fit World Club Championship regulations in 2005?

27-Who gave up the number 11 for Mo Salah when he joined the club?

28-Which Liverpool player had to change his shirt name when promoted to the premier league with Wolves?

29-What current Liverpool player made his name playing as a defensive midfielder for Brazilian club Figueirense?

30-Who does Van Dijk nickname "Flaco"?

PLAYERS

31-What current Spanish red has a brother who plays for Brazil ?

32-How old was Salah when he scored his first goal for Egypt ?

33-What did Ian Rush do to mark his 600th game for Liverpool?

34.What Player was a commentator in the first season of the Indian Super League?

35.Who is the only Liverpool player to score in a league cup final, champions league final , UEFA CUP final and FA Cup final?

36.Who Is the highest scoring African player in Liverpool's history?

37-What current player shares a birthday with all time appearance holder Ian Callaghan ?

38-What Liverpool player dropped their phone of the 18/19 Champions league tour bus?

39-When getting married in Argentine in 2013 who invited the entire village to the ceremony?

40-What Ex-Liverpool player claimed he was "The best in the world" after taking his country to a world cup final?

PLAYERS

31-What current Spanish red has a brother who plays for Brazil?

32-How old was Salah when he scored his first goal for Egypt?

33-What did Ian Rush do to mark his 600th game for Liverpool?

34.What Player was a commentator in the first season of the Indian Super League?

35.Who is the only Liverpool player to score in a league cup final, champions league final , UEFA CUP final and FA Cup final?

36.Who Is the highest scoring African player in Liverpool's history?

37-What current player shares a birthday with all time appearance holder Ian Callaghan?

38-What Liverpool player dropped their phone of the 18/19 Champions league tour bus?

39-When getting married in Argentine in 2013 who invited the entire village to the ceremony?

40-What Ex-Liverpool player claimed he was "The best in the world" after taking his country to a world cup final?

PLAYERS

41-Kolo Toure was known as a player who always had a smile on his face but after a slow start at Liverpool who did he score his debut goal against?

42-How many players in the current squad (21/22) have won the Liverpool player of the year award?

43-Who is the longest serving Liverpool player?

44-In the premier league era, what player has had the most red cards in the league?

45-Who has kept the most clean sheets for Liverpool?

46-Who is the youngest player to play for Liverpool?

47-What current player started his career at Ligue 1 team Metz?
48-In the premier league era what player has had the most league wins?

49-Who's won the most Liverpool player of the year awards since 2002?

50-What player is known for doing "Spaghetti legs" ?

51-How many Liverpool players have scored on all 7 days of the week?

CAPTAINS

1.Who is the current Liverpool captain (As of 2022) ?

2. Which Ex-liverpool captain has managed Rangers and Aston Villa since retiring?

3.In the 2015-16 season Liverpool used their highest number of captains, but how many did they have?

4.During the 2021/21 how many people captained Liverpool?

5.Who is the only Liverpool captain to win the Premier league?

6.What season was Steven Gerrard made captain?

7.How many people have captained Liverpool once?

8.How many league titles did Donald Mckinlay win with Liverpool?

9.-Who did Liverpool buy Sami Hyypia from?

10.Who was Jordan Henderson's first game as captain?

CAPTAINS

11.Who did Alan Hansen sign for Liverpool from?

12.What player has had the most games as captain?

13-How many appearances did Alex Raisbeck make for Liverpool?

14-How many goals did Steven Gerrard score for Liverpool?

15-What London team did Graeme Souness start his career with?

16-How many Fa cups did Tommy Smith win with Liverpool ?

17-How long did Ron Yeats play for Liverpool for?

18-How many trophies did Liverpool win during Emlyn Hughes's reign as captain?

19-What Liverpool captain was added to the Premier league hall of fame?

20-How long did it take Ron Yeats to be appointed captain?

CAPTAINS

21- Who had the most games as Liverpool captain?

22-How much did Emlyn Hughes sign for Liverpool for?

23-Who was Liverpool's first captain?

24-How old was Steven Gerrard when he was appointed as captain?

25- Who was the captain for Liverpool's first FA Cup title?

26-Who was Ian Rush's testimonial against?

27-Who was Liverpool captain for longest?

28-How did Emlyn Hughes become Liverpool captain?

29-Who was Steven Gerrards testimonial against?

30-Where is current Liverpool captain Jordan Henderson from?

CAPTAINS

31-What was unique about Phil Babb's game as captain?

32-How many league titles did Graeme Souness win with Liverpool?

33-When did Ron Yeats leave Liverpool?

34-Whos short reign as captain was ended when Steven Gerrard was given the armband?

35-How many games was Graeme Souness captain for?

36-Who was Alan Hansen's testimonial against?

37 How many champions leagues did Alan Hansen win with Liverpool?

38.In 1964 who did Liverpool sign Emlyn Hughes from?

39.In 2011 Liverpool's Jordan Henderson signed for Liverpool but how much did he cost?

40.How many Europa Leagues did Emlyn Hughes win with Liverpool?

CAPTAINS

41-How many trophies did Liverpool win while Ron Yeats was captain?

42-How many years after joining Liverpool did Graeme Souness become captain?

43-Who was Gerrard's first game as Liverpool captain?

44-What Liverpool captain was nicknamed "Crazy Horse"?

45-Who was Billy Dunlop's testimonial against?

46-How many trophies did Liverpool win while Gerrard was captain?

47-Since his retirement what is Alan Hansen now known for?

48-Who appointed Steven Gerrard as captain?

49-Who did Paisley give Souness the armband from, starting a rivalry between the two players?

50-Who was Emlyn Hughes's testimonial against?

ANFIELD

1.What is the capacity of Anfield?

2. When was Anfield built?

3.What was the record attendance at Anfield?

4.What are the four stands named ?

5.True or false, Anfield is the 5th biggest stadium in England?

6.What other team have used Anfield as their home ground?

7.Who did Liverpool play their first league match at Anfield against?

8.How many people attended the first match?

9.When were the Shankly gates erected?

10.What is Liverpool's longest home unbeaten run?

ANFIELD

11.What ground lies just half a mile away, separated only by Stanley Park?

12.Who installed the "This is Anfield" sign?

13-What song do Liverpool fans sing at the start of home matches?

14-What current Liverpool player is unbeaten in the premier league at Anfield?

15-Which two former managers have gates named after them?

16-Which stand is currently being extended and is due to be completed in time for the 2023/24 season?

17-What will the capacity be following this extension?

18-What was the first game played at Anfield?

19-When were floodlights first installed at Anfield?

20-When was Bill Shankly's statue erected?

ANFIELD

21- When was Bob Paisley's statue erected?

22-What are people who sit in the Kop known as?

23-What is the oldest stand in Anfield?

24-What trophy that Paisley won three times is depicted in his gate?

25- Who's plans to build a new stadium were abandoned following the sale of the club?

26.What was the first international match played at Anfield?

27.When did Liverpool women first play at Anfield and who did they play?

28.How many fa cup semi-finals has Anfield hosted?

29.When was the last time a Fa cup semi-final was hosted at Anfield?

30.When was the most recent international match played at the ground?

ANFIELD

31. In 1971 what rival played a home game at Anfield?

32. In the summer of 2019 who performed at Anfield?

33. Who is set to perform at Anfield in the summer of 2022?

34. Who was hired in 1906 to design the new Anfield?

35. When Shankly took over what was the average attendance at Anfield?

36. How many seats are in the main stand?

37. Which owners decided upon expanding Anfield after buying the club in 2010?

38. How many rugby matches has the stadium hosted?

39. Who opened the Shankly Gates?

40. Who named the kop?

ANFIELD

41. A flagpole was erected beside the kop but what is unique about how it was obtained?

42 What's the capacity of the Anfield Road End?

43. The Kop was finished in 2016 but where does the lower section date back to?

44. In 1984 what was unique about an American performer tbat attracted crowds of over 30,000 for a whole week to Anfield ?

45. What season was the highest average attendance at Anfield?

46. What is the most consecutive league wins at Anfield?

47. What's the capacity of the Kop?

48. How many games did Liverpool win in their longest unbeaten streak at Anfield in 1978-1981?

49. What is the closest train station to Anfield?

50. What's the capacity of the Sir Kenny Dalglish stand?

FAMOUS GAMES

1.How did Liverpool win the 2005 Champions league final?

2. The first ever game on Match of The day was Liverpool vs who?

3.The first ever game televised in colour was Liverpool vs who?

4.How many Champions league finals have Liverpool been in?

5.What was historic about the date Liverpool played the Champions league final against Spurs?

6.True or false, Liverpool are the only club to contest a major final in three countries in mainland Britain?

7.Liverpool have scored 21 goals in Fa Cup finals, how many of those came in the first half?

8.What surprising player got the assist for Origi's goal in the 2018/19 Champions league final?

9.Where was the 2018/19 Champions league final held?

10.Who scored the winning goal in Liverpool's comeback against Borussia Dortmund in the 2015/16 season?

FAMOUS GAMES

11. Who score the winning goal to take Liverpool to the 2018/19 Champions league final in a 4-0 comeback against Barcelona?

12.Liverpool have won the most Champions league trophies on penalties but how many times have they been sent to spot kicks?

13-Who did Liverpool beat in the Champions League final at their own ground?

14-How many points did Liverpool get in the 1989/90 title winning season?

15-What was unique about the 1975/76 UEFA cup final?

16-Who scored the winning goal in the 2-1 win over Chelsea in the 2006 Community Shield?

17-Liverpool have only won five major trophies without a player from what country in the squad?

18-How many times have Liverpool won the Fa cup?

19-Liverpool's youngest starting line up was recorded as 19 years and 182 days in the league cup against Aston Villa, why was the starting team so young ?

20-What was Liverpools biggest League cup win?

FAMOUS GAMES

21-Who did Liverpool beat on penalties in the 2011/2 league cup final?

22-Liverpool won the 21/22 league cup but who was their top goal scorer in the competition?

23-How many goals did he score throughout the competition?

24- Who did Liverpool beat in the 2019 Club World Cup Final to win their first of the trophy?

25- What was Liverpool's biggest European cup (Champions league) win ?

26-How long did it take for Paul Walsh to score at Anfield against West Ham in 1984?

27-Who beat Manchester City to confirm Liverpool as premier league winners for the first time in 2019/20?

28-Who was the last player to score in their last match for Liverpool ?

29-Who scored the winner in the 1980/81 Champions league final?

30-The 2001 Community Shield wasn't held at its usual ground Wembley, where was it held?

FAMOUS GAMES

31-Why wasn't the 2001 Community Shield held at Wembley?

32 How many times have Liverpool won the League cup?

33-In Liverpools premier league winning season who was the top goal scorer?

34-How did Liverpool win the 2019/20 Super cup?

35-Who has scored the most hattricks for Liverpool?

36-Who scored the winning goal in the 2000/01 Fa Cup final?

37-How many community Shields have Liverpool won?

38-What was Liverpool's biggest league win?

39-What did Liverpool's 2-1 over AC Milan in December 2021 mean?

40-What type of goal gifted Liverpool the UEFA Cup in 2001?

FAMOUS GAMES

41-Who did Liverpool beat in their first Fa Cup final in 1965?

42-How many players have scored for Liverpool in the club's history?

43-Who is Liverpool's all time Champions league top goal scorer?

44-On what attempt did Liverpool win their first Fa Cup?

45-What is interesting about 5 of Liverpool's community Shield trophies?

46-Who did Liverpool play in the 2005/06 Fa Cup Final?

47-Who was the oldest player to debut for Liverpool?

48-Who has made the most appearances in the Champions league for Liverpool?

49-Who was Liverpool's 5000th game against?

50-Who's had the most assists in one season for Liverpool?

RIVALRIES

1.Who are Liverpool's city rivals?

2. Who are Liverpool's biggest non city rival?

3.One Liverpool player is the only player to score a hattrick at Old Trafford in the premier league, who is it?

4.Which Balon dor winner left Liverpool for their biggest rivals?

5.What Ex-Liverpool captain famously managed Manchester United?

6.What Ex-Liverpool player joined city rivals Everton in 1991?

7.Who was the first player to win the FA Cup with both Liverpool and Everton?

8.Who is the only player to appear for both Liverpool and Everton in merseyside derbies in the same season?

9.What team have Liverpool drawn the most times in the Fa Cup?

10.Which Ex Liverpool and Manchester United players are now unlikely friends since becoming tv pundits?

RIVALRIES

11.Until recently what Liverpool player lived in Manchester United legend Ole Gunnar Solskjaer's house?

13-What German goalkeeper played for both Man City and Liverpool?

14-What team has Milner made more appearances, Man City or Liverpool?

15-What is ironic about the Liverpool,Everton derby being referred to as "The Friendly derby"?

16-What is the derby with Manchester United known as?

17-What rival team did Liverpool's first captain Andrew Hannah play for?

18-How many players have played for both Liverpool and Manchester United?

19-Who has the most clean sheets against Everton?

20-How many official games has there been between Liverpool and Everton?

RIVALRIES

21-How many players have moved from Liverpool to Everton?

22-In the 2018/19 season who scored the iconic winner at Anfield over Everton?

23-Games against what other Liverpool side count as "Merseyside Derbies"?

24-Who is Liverpools top goal scorer against Everton?

25- How many goals has he scored against Everton?

26-How many games was the longest unbeaten run against Everton?

27-How many players have moved from Everton to Liverpool?

28-What was the highest attendance between Liverpool and Everton?

29-How many players has Liverpool bought from Manchester United?

30-How many friendlies have Liverpool played against Everton?

RIVALRIES

31-How many official games have Liverpool played against Manchester United?

32-How many penalties have Liverpool been awarded at Goodison Park since the second war?

33-What is Liverpools biggest win against Everton?

34-How many players have played for Liverpool,Everton and Tranmere Rovers?

35-Who is Liverpool's top goal scorer against Manchester United?

36-How many players have scored for both Liverpool and Everton in Mersey derbies?

37-How many times have Liverpool done the double (won both league games in a season) against Everton?

38-Who has the most appearances against Everton?

39-How many testimonials have been between Everton and Liverpool?

40-In 1986-87 Liverpool played Everton more times than any other season but how many times did they play?

RIVALRIES

41. How many of these games did Liverpool win?

42- How many players has Liverpool sold players to Manchester United?

43- How many times has Liverpool played Manchester United in European competitions?

44- Who was the last person to have a testimonial against Everton?

45- What were Manchester United called the first time Liverpool played them?

46. Why did Liverpool play an away game against Manchester United at their other rivals ground Goodison Park in 1948?

47. How many players have played for both Liverpool and Everton?

48. How many times have Liverpool women played Manchester United women?

49- How many times have Liverpool beat Everton three times in a season?

50- What Evertonian became a Manchester United legend and all-time top goalscorer furthering his rivalry with the reds?

1892-1900

1. What colour did Liverpool play before they played in red?

2. Who was the first player to ever score for Liverpool?

3. Who founded Liverpool?

4. What were Liverpool fc initially called?

5. What was the score of Liverpool's first friendly match?

6. What was notable about Liverpools first starting 11?

7. What did Liverpool win in the 1893-94 season?

8. After Liverpool were promoted to the First Division in 1896, who was appointed as manager?

9. Where was Tom Watson from?

10. Who scored Liverpools first ever goal?

1892-1900

11.Who was Liverpools 100th game against?

12.When is Liverpools official birthday?

13-Who did Tom Watson manage before Liverpool?

14-Who did Liverpool win their first league match against?

15-When did John Houlding break away from the board of Everton?

16-What was the score of Liverpools first official match?

17-Who did Liverpool play in their first official match?

18-Why did Liverpool change their name to Liverpool?

19-In 1986 Liverpool made a record league win of what score?

20-Who was Liverpools first manager?

1892-1900

21- Who scored Liverpool's 100th goal?

22-Who replaced Liverpool's first manager in 1895?

23-Where was Liverpool's first manager from?

24-When was Tom Watson appointed as manager?

25- How many spells did John Mckenna have as Liverpool chairman?

26-How many league titles did Tom Watson win with Sunderland?

27-Who recruited Tom Watson?

28-Who else did William Edward Barclay manage?

29-When was William Edward Barclay born?

30-Who was John McKenna's first signing?

1892-1900

31-Who did Liverpool battle with to win the Lancashire league in their inaugural season?

32-How many major honours did Tom Watson win?

33-What was the score of Liverpool's 50th game?

34-What coincided with Tom Watson's first game as manager?

35-Who was Liverpool's top goalscorer in their first season ?

36-How many goals did he score?

37-How many games did John Mckenna manage?

38-Who did Harry Bradshaw sign from?

39-How many attempts does it take Liverpool to get promoted to the first division?

40-Where was John Mckenna from?

1892-1900

41-Who was the top goalscorer of the 1894/95 season?

42-How many players were bought in Liverpools first season?

43-How did Liverpool convince Tom Watson to manage Liverpool?

44-Two players made 31 appearances for Liverpool in the 1893/94, who were they?

45-Who was John McKenna's last signing?

46-Who scored Liverpools 500th Goal?

47-After being given £500 where did William Edward Barclay go to scout players?

48-Who did Liverpool play in their 250th game?

49-Who was William Edward Barclays last signing?

50-What was the score of Liverpools 250th game?

1901-1910

1. Liverpool won their first league title in 1900/01 but who was the top goal scorer?

2. Who scored Liverpools 1000th goal?

3.Who was the first player Liverpool bought in the 1900's ?
4.-Where did he sign from?

5.How many times did Liverpool win the second division between 1901-1910?

6.-Where was Billy Dunlop from?

7.-In 1904 who did Bobby Robinson make his debut against?

8.-How many games did Tom Watson manage?

9.-Who signed for Liverpool in 1904 from Sunderland?

10.What was the transfer fee?

1901-1910

11.Between 1901-1910 how many league titles did Liverpool win?

12-Where did Alex Raidbeck sign from?

13-What year did Bobby Robinson score his most goals?

14-Who did Jack Cox play his last game against?

15-Who was Tom Watson's record signing?

16-How many games did Billy Dunlop play for Liverpool?

17-How many years after joining the football league did it take Liverpool to win the first division?

18-Who did Jack Cox join Liverpool from(Blackpool)

19-How many caps did Billy Dunlop have for Scotland (1)

20-How much did Liverpool sign Arthur Goddard for (£460)

1901-1910

21- How many games did Bobby Robinson play for Liverpool?

22-How many league games did Tom Watson manage?

23-How many games did Jack Cox play for Liverpool?

24-How many goals did Billy Dunlop score for Liverpool?

25- Sam Raybould was the top goal scorer of the 1902/03 season but how many goals did he score?

26-How many international caps did Alex Raisbeck have?

27-Where did Liverpool sign Sam Hardy from?

28-In 1904 who did Bobby Robinson score his first goal against?

29-How many goals did Sam Raybould score under Tom Watson?

30-Which player that signed for Liverpool in 1898 is now part of the Liverpool hall of fame?

1901-1910

31-How many goals did Jack Cox score for Liverpool?

32-In his best goalscoring season how many goals did Bobby Robinson score?

33-Who made the most appearances under Tom Watson?

34-How many appearances did he make?

35-Who did Sam Hardy make his 100th appearance against?

36-How many clean sheets did Sam Hardy keep?

37-Who was Billy Dunlop's 250th appearance against?

38-How many appearances did Jack Cox make for Liverpool?

39-How many penalties did Bobby Robinson score?

40-Billy Dunlop's final Liverpool goal was a 90th minute finish in a 4-1 win over who?

1901-1910

41-Which season did Sam Hardy keep his most clean sheets?

42-Who scored the most goals under Tom Watson?

43-How much did Liverpool sign Sam Hardy for?

44-Who did Sam Hardy make his debut against?

45-Who did Bobby Robinson score his most goals against?

46-How many goals did he score against them?

47-How much did Sam Raybould sign for Liverpool for?

48-How many clean sheets did Sam Hardy keep in his best season?

49-How many games did Maurice Parry play for Liverpool?

50-Who was Billy Dunlops final appearance against?

1911-1920

1. Who did Liverpool play in their first Fa cup final?

2. -Who did Sam Hardy play his 250th appearance against?

3.Who did Bobby Robinson score his final goal against?

4.-Who did Liverpool sign from Leyton in 1910?

5.-Who made their last appearance in 1911 against Gainsborough Trinity?

6.-Who made the most appearances of the 1911-12 season?

7. How many appearances did he make that season?

8. Who was appointed Liverpool manager in 1918?

9.Who did Bobby Robinson play his 250th game against?

10.How many appearances did Alf West make for Liverpool?

1911-1920

11.-How many appearances did Ephraim Longworth make for Liverpool?

12.-Who made 34 of his 39 Liverpool appearances in the 1915/16 season?

13-What did the Liverpool Echo include an article about in 1918?

14-What club did Ephraim Longworth make the most appearances against?

15-How many appearances did he make?

16- Who was Jack Parkinson's final appearance against?

17-What was unique when Alf West left Barnsley for Liverpool?

18-In 1914 Tom Watson made his last signing, who was it?
19-Who did he sign from?

20-When did Bob Ferguson sign for Liverpool ?

1911-1920

21- Though his time was short with the club, what was notable about it?

22-Jack Parkinson scored his final Liverpool goal in a 2-1 win over who?

23-Who was Bob Ferguson the captain for when Liverpool signed him?

24-How many appearances did Donald Mckinlay make?

25- Who was George Patterson's first signing?

26-Who scored his last goal of an iconic career in 1913 against Bolton?

27-Who was described as "Not a brilliant forward, but a useful one"?

28- Who described him in this way?

29-How many clubs had Tom Watson worked at before Liverpool?

30-Who made his debut appearance against Sheffield united in 1910 ?

1911-1920

31-Who played 49 games for Liverpool as a wartime guest in 1915?

32- Who made his most appearances against merseyside rivals Everton?

33-Jack Parkinson's 100th goal came at Anfield in a game against who in 1911?

34-How long did Donald Mckinlay spend at Liverpool?

35-How many goals did Jimmy Nicholl score in his short time at the club?

36-How many games did Ken Campbell play for Liverpool?

37-Who scored the most goals of the 1917-18 season?

38-How many players did George Patterson sell?

39-Who did Donald Mckinlay join Liverpool from?

40-Who did Ephraim Longworth play his 200th appearance against

1911-1920

41-Who was described as a "Typical Scottish half-back, neat and clever"?

42-In 1909/10 who won the First division top scorer?

43 Who did Ken Campbell play both his debut and 50th game against?

44-How many league games did Tom Watson win as manager?

45-Who was George Patterson's last signing?

46-How many clean sheets did Ken Campbell keep?

47- How old was Tom Watson when appointed manager?

48-How many wartime appearances did Ephraim Longworth make?

49-Who did Bob Ferguson make his 100th appearance against?

50-Jack Parkinson's 200th appearance in 1913 came against who?

1921-1930

1. Who was Liverpool's 1000th game against?

2. What years did Liverpool win consecutive league titles?

3.In 1928 what upgrade did Anfield receive?

4.Who returned in their 1928 for their second spell as manager?

5.Who Scored Liverpool's 2000th goal?

6.-Who made the most appearances under Matt McQueen?

7.15 years after the player left the club who was described as?

8.Who was the last signing of Matt McQueen's reign?

9.How many games did Patterson manage in his second term?

10.-Who did Ephraim Longworth make his final appearance against?

1921-1930

11.-What did Matt McQueen do before managing Liverpool?

12-How many appearances did Walter Wadsworth make?

13-Who made the most appearances of the 1922-23 season?

14-Who was the first signing of Matt McQueen's reign?

15-How many years did Ephraim Longworth play for Liverpool?

16-Who scored the most goals under Matt McQueen?

17-Who did the Liverpool Echo say was "One of the hardest nuts an opposing forward can expect to meet"?

18-When was Matt McQueen born?

19-True or False Ephraim Longworth is now inducted into the Liverpool Hall of fame?

20-How many penalties did Harry Chambers score?

1921-1930

21- How many appearances did Tommy Lucas make for Liverpool?

22-Where is Matt McQueen from?

23-What did Ephraim Longworth do when he retired?

24-George Patterson was the first of two Liverpool managers to return for a second term in the job, but in 2011 who followed Patterson's footsteps, returning to Anfield for the second time?

25- What rival team did Tommy Lucas play for as a wartime guest?

26 How many appearances did Harry Chambers make for Liverpool?

27-Who did James Jackson make his 100th appearance against?

28-Where was Elisha Scott from?

29-How many games did Matt McQueen manage?

30-Who did Walter Wadsworth play his 100th game against?

1921-1930

31-How many caps did Elisha Scott make for Northern Ireland?

32-How many goals did Harry Chambers score for Liverpool?

33-Who did Tommy Lucas make his 250th appearance against?

34-How many players did Matt McQueen sign?

35-Who was the top goal scorer of the 1923/24 season?

36 How many appearances did James Jackson make for Liverpool?

37-How many wartime games did Elisha Scott play?

38-How many trophies did Matt McQueen win?

39-Who did Tommy Lucas make the most appearances against?

40-How many appearances did he make against them?

1921-1930

41-Who did James Jackson sign for Liverpool from?

42-How many appearances did Tom Bromilow make for Liverpool?

43-Who did Jimmy Walsh sign from?

44 Who did Harry Chambers score his most goals against?

45 How many goals did he score?

46-What did James Jackson do when he retired?

47-How many players did Matt McQueen sell?

48 How much did Liverpool pay for James Jackson?

49- Who did Tom Bromilow make the most appearances against?

50-How many appearances did he make against them?

1931-1940

1. How many games did George Kay manage?

2. Who said, "George Kay was a first-class manager and a very big influence on me"?

3.-Who made the most appearances of George Kay's reign?

4.- Who did Berry Nieuwenhuys make his debut against?

5.-How many appearances did Matt Busby make?

6.Who did Jack Balmer score Liverpool's fastest goal against?

7.-Who was the top goal scorer of the 1931-32 season?

8.-How many goals did he score?

9.Who did Tiny Bradshaw make his most appearances against?

10.Who was George Patterson's last signing?

1931-1940

11.Who scored the most goals of George Kay's reign?

12-How many goals did he score?

13- What legendary Manchester United manager did George Patterson sign from Manchester City?

14-How many games did Gordon Hodgson play for Liverpool?

15-How many players did George Kay sign?

16-Where was Jack Balmer from?

17-When was George Kay's first game as manage?

18-Who said "The Manager, George Kay wasn't a bad fella either. You'd never hear him cursing and swearing"?

19- Who was George Kay's first signing?

20- How many league games did George Kay manage?

1931-1940

21- Who did Jack Balmer score the most goals against?

22-How many did he score against the club?

23-How many signings did George Patterson made in his second spell at the club?

24-Who was George Kay's record signing?

25- Who did he sign from?

26-Who did George Kay manage before Liverpool?

27-How many penalties did Jack Balmer score?

28-What other clubs did George Kay manage?

29-Who did Jack Balmer have his 100th appearance against?

30-How many trophies did George Kay win?

1931-1940

30-How many trophies did George Kay win?

31-Who did Phil Taylor sign for Liverpool from?

32-How much did Liverpool spend on Matt Busby?

33-How many appearances did Tom Cooper make for Liverpool?

34-Where was George Kay from?

35-How many caps did Tom Cooper make for his country?

36-Where was Matt Busby from?

37-Where was Phil Taylor from?

38-Who did Eddie Spicer have his testimonial against?

39-Who did Tiny Bradshaw play both his debut and 50th game against?

40-What trophies did George Kay win?

1931-1940

41-How many players did George Kay Sell?

42-How many appearances did Tiny Bradshaw make for Liverpool?

43-Where did Liverpool sign Tom Cooper from?

44-What two teams did Eddie spicer make his most appearances against?

45-How many appearances did he make?

46-Who did Liverpool sign Gordon Hodgson from?

47-How many appearances did Eddie Spicer make for Liverpool?

48-What did the Liverpool Echo say Matt Busby's greatest strength on the field?

49-What was Ironic about Tiny Bradshaw's nickname as Tiny?

50 How many goals did Gordon Hodgson score?

1941-1950

1. In 1946 Liverpool broke the transfer fee spending £12,500 on who?

2. -Who took the captaincy from Jack Balmer in 1949/50?

3.Who was the first Liverpool to score in three consecutive hat-tricks?

4.Who did he score them against?

5.-How many international caps did Phil Taylor make?

6-What did Phil Taylor do when he retired?

7.Where did Laurie Hughes sign from?

8.How many trophies did Phil Taylor win?

9.How many games did bob Paisley play for Liverpool?

10-Who did George Kay manage before Liverpool?

1941-1950

11. How many war time games did Bob Paisley play?

12. Who did Laurie Hughes play his first game against?

13. How many clean sheets did Cyril Sidlow keep?

14. Who did Jack Balmer score his 100th goal against?

15. How many international caps did Ray Lambert have for Wales?

16. How many goals did Bob Paisley score for Liverpool?

17. Liverpool won the 1947 league title finishing one point ahead of who?

18. Which Liverpool player became manager in 1956?

19. How much did Liverpool pay for Cyril Sidlow?

20. Who was George Kay's last signing?

1941-1950

21- How many appearances did Berry Nieuwenhuys make?

22-How many games did Laurie Hughes play for Liverpool?

23-Who did Ray Lambert make his debut against?

24-What year did Liverpool first visit Wembley?

25- Who did they play in their first visit?

26-How many war time games did Ray Lambert play?

27-Where did Liverpool buy Bob Paisley from?

28-Who did Berry Nieuwenhuys make the most appearances against?

29-Who did Liverpool play in Laurie Hughes 100th appearance?

30-How many international caps did Cyril Sidlow make?

1941-1950

31- How many games did Ray Lambert play?

32-Where was Berry Nieuwenhuys from?

33-How many goals did Laurie Hughes score for Liverpool?

34-What did Bob Paisley say he was training to become towards the end of his career?

35-Who was dubbed the "Merseyside Matthews"?

36-Who scored 147 war time goals in 137 games for Liverpool?

37-Who did Ray Lambert make his most Liverpool appearances against ?

38-How many games did he play against them?

39-What competition did Bob Paisley debut in?

40-Who did Berry Nieuwenhuys make his 250th appearance against?

1941-1950

41-How many goals did Ray Lambert score?

42-Who did Bob Paisley make the most appearances against ?

43-Who did Jimmy Payne make his debut against?

44-Cyril Done scored 4 goals against two teams, who were they?

45-Who did Ray Lambert play his 150th appearance against ?

46-Stubbins scored his joint most goals against 5 teams, what teams were they?

47-How many goals did he score against these teams?

48- How many appearances did Jimmy Payne make for Liverpool?

49-Who did Jimmy Payne score his debut goal against?

50-Who did Bob Paisley make his 100th appearance against?

1951-1960

1. When was Bill Shankly appointed manager?

2. How many players did Bill Shankly release when he was appointed?

3.What room did Shankly turn into a room where coaches would discuss strategy?

4.Who was Liverpool's 2000th game against?

5.- "I'm a people's man- only the people matter." Who said this?

6.-Where was Ronnie Moran from?

7.-Who was the top goalscorer in Phil Taylors reign?

8.-Who was Ronnie Moran's last goal against?

9-What type of goal was it?

10.Who did Bill Shankly manage before Liverpool?

1951-1960

11.-Where was Tommy Younger from?

12- What ex player was appointed manager in 1956?

13- Bill Shankly spent 17 years playing for what club?

14-How many players did Bill Shankly buy?

15-Where did Tommy Younger sign from?

16-How many games did Ronnie Moran play for Liverpool?

17-What did all of Bill Shankly's brothers have in common?

18-After taking a break from football what job did Phil Taylor do?

19-What did Shankly say he specialised in as a footballer?

20-Who recommended Ronnie Moran to Liverpool's chairman ?

1951-1960

21- What competition did Liverpool make their record Anfield attendance?

22-Where was Don Welsh from?

23-Who made the most appearances under Phil Taylor?

24-Who was Bill Shankly's first signing?

25- How many signings did Don Welsh sign?

26-Who was Phil Taylor's record signing?

27-What future Liverpool legend said that Ronnie Moran was his idol?

28-How much was Don Welsh paid as manager?

29-Who did Ronnie Moran make his debut against?

30-Where did Liverpool buy john Molyneux from?

1951-1960

31-When was Phil Taylor appointed?

32-Did Bill Shankly ever play for Liverpool?

33-How many games did Don Welsh manage?

34- Who did John Molyneux make his debut against?

35-Who was Ronnie Moran's 100th Liverpool game against?

36-Where is Phil Taylor from?

37-Who did Liverpool play in Laurie Hughes 250th appearance?

38-How many goals did Ronnie Moran score for Liverpool?

39-How many players did Don Welsh sell?

40-Who was Laurie Hughes last appearance against?

1951-1960

41-What other clubs did Don Welsh manage ?

42-What other sport did Bill Shankly participate in?

43 How many people did Phil Taylor sell?

44-What did Don Welsh do after leaving Liverpool?

45-What was notable about Phil Taylor's reign?

46-Who did John Molyneux play his 100th goal against?

47-How many players did Phil Taylor buy ?

48-Who did Laurie Hughes score his debut goal against?

49-Who did Don Welsh manage when appointed by Liverpool?

50-Who did John Molyneux score his first goal against?

1961-1970

1. Liverpool were promoted back into the first division in 1961 but when did they win their next league title?

2. In 1965 what did Liverpool win for the first time?

3. What song did Liverpool fans begin to sing before matches in the 1960's?

4. Who was the last player to move between Liverpool and Manchester United, moving in 1964?

5. Who scored Liverpool's 5000th goal?

6. What player that signed in 1968 had the most clean sheets of any Liverpool goalkeeper?

7. What player that signed in 1961 was known as the Saint?

8. How much was the Saint signed for?

9. Who else did Shankly sign in 1961?

10. What did the two signings have in common?

1961-1970

11. What did Bill Shankly claim about Ron Yeats?

12.In 1962 Liverpool were promoted to the first division with how many games to spare?

13-Who did Liverpool beat 2-0 to confirm promotion?

14-In 1964 what did Bill Shankly do that he thought would intimidate the opposition?

15-In 1964 Liverpool made their debut in what type of football?

16-Who did Liverpool play in their European cup (Champions league) debut?

17-In 1964 Liverpool won the time, how many did titles did they have by 1964?

18-What did the score end in Liverpool's first European tie(Over both legs)?

19-In 1964 why were the turnstiles shut an hour before a game against Arsenal?

20-Who did the reds beat 2-1 in their first Fa Cup title win?

1961-1970

21- Who scored in the 2-1 win?

22-In 1964 Liverpool draw 2-2 in the charity shield, sharing it with who?

23-What did bill Shankly do before a European cup tie to fire up the Kop?

24-In 1965 who did Liverpool share their second consecutive FA Cup with?

25- What world cup winner scored the winning goal in a 1-0 to win the 1966 Community Shield?

26-Who did the reds play in the 1966 Community Shield?

27-Who got the assist for Ian St johns 1965 Fa cup final winning goal?

28-What goalkeeper has had the most appearances for Liverpool?

29-Who made the most appearances under Bill Shankly?

30-Who was Ian Callaghan's 50th appearance against?

1961-1970

31-How many international caps did Ian Callaghan have?

32 Where did Ian St John join Liverpool from?

33-A 5-0 win over who confirmed the 1963 league title?

34-Who scored the most goals under Bill Shankly?

35-Ian Callaghan has played the most games for Liverpool of any player, but how many games did he play?

36-In the 1966 title win, how many players did Liverpool use?

37-After returning from a knee operation what position did Bill Shankly move Callaghan into?

38 How many goals did John Molyneux play for Liverpool?

39-In 1966 Liverpool played their first European cup final but who did they play?

40-How many years did it take the club to win their first Fa Cup?

1961-1970

41-What was unique about the 1966 Community Shield win?

42-How long after the world cup was Ian Callaghan given his winners medal?

43-Who said "Ian Callaghan is everything good that a man can be. No praise is too high for him" ?

44-How many goals did Ian Callaghan score for Liverpool?

45-When did John Molyneux play his final game?

46-How many league games did Shankly manage for Liverpool?

47-Who was Ian Callaghan's 250th appearance against?

48 What was the score of the first European game at Anfield?

49-How many games did John Molyneux play for Liverpool?

50-Who was Liverpools first signing of the 70's?

1971-1980

1. Which legendary striker signed for a world record fee of £300,000 in 1980?

2. Starting in 1974 and ending in 1983 who played 417 games in a row for the club?

3. What did Liverpool win in the 1972-73 season?

4. Who replaced Shankly as manager in 1975?

5. What did Paisley win in his second season as manager?

6. In 1977 what did Liverpool win for the first time?

7. What was the only trophy Bob Paisley failed to win?

8. How many consecutive league cups did Bob Paisley win?

9. Who was Liverpools first kit manufacturer in 1973?

10-Who is Liverpool's highest assister?

1971-1980

11. In 1974 Liverpool beat Stromsgodset 11-0 but how many goal scorers were there?

12. Despite losing the 1971 Fa Cup final, what was significant about the day?

13- What Liverpool player has scored the most goals after coming on as a sub?

14- Who did Liverpool beat in a three way battle for the title in 1973?

15- Who did Liverpool beat to win their first UEFA Cup?

16- Who was Liverpool's first Shirt sponsor in 1979?

17- What was the score over two legs in the 1973 UEFA Cup win?

18- In 1974 Liverpool won the Fa Cup, beating who in the final?

19- What was the score in the 1974 Fa Cup final?

20- In 1980 who is the first player to be named PFA player of the year/

1971-1980

21- Liverpool win their fifth Charity Shield in a row beating which second division team?

22-Liverpool win their 12th title beating who 4-1 at Anfield?

23-What year did Bill Shankly retire?

24-Who scored in the 1979 Community Shield win over Arsenal?

25- Who scored in a 3-1 win over Wolves to confirm Liverpools 9th league title?

26-What score at Anfield saw Liverpool secure the European Super cup over Kevin Keegan's Hambury?

27-Who did Liverpool beat on goal difference to win the 1976 league title?

28-What score saw Liverpool share the community Shield with rivals Manchester United in 1977?

29-Where did Liverpool win their 1977 European Cup?

30-Who walked Liverpool out in the 1974 Community Shield?

1971-1980

31-What Supersub saw Liverpool beat Saint-Etienne 1-0?

32-Who did Liverpool beat in the 1976 UEFA Cup final?

33-Where did Liverpool play in the 1966 European cup final?

34-What was the aggregate score in the 1976 UEFA Cup win?

35-Who did Liverpool beat in the 1974 fa cup final?

36-How did Bill Shankly announce his retirement?

37-How did Liverpool win the 1974 community shield?

38-How many matches were played under Bill Shanklys reign?

39-How many trophies did Bill Shankly win?

40-When was Bob Paisley born?

1971-1980

41-Who did Liverpool beat in the 1974 Community Shield?

42-Who said the quote "Some people believe football is a matter of life and death, I am very disappointed with that attitude. I can assure you it is much, much more important than that"?

43-What year was Bill Shankly born?

44-In August 1976 Liverpool won the Community Shield again but who scored in the 1-0 win against Southampton?

45-Liverpool retain the European cup, beating who at Wembly?

46-Who scored the winning goal in the 1978 European cup win?

47-Liverpool's 11th title sees them set a first division points record, but how many points did they achieve?

48-In 1977 Liverpool won their 10th title, winning how many of their 21 games at Anfield?

49-In 1977 Liverpool win their first European cup, but who scored in the 3-1 final win?

50-In 1977 Kenny Dalglish signs from what club?

1981-1990

1. What team changed goalkeepers three times during a 3-3 draw with the reds in 1982?

2. In 1989 Liverpool Women's team was formed but what were they called?

3. How many times did Liverpool win the European cup (Champions league) between 1981-1990?

4. How many Liverpool players won the football Writers footballer of the year between 1981-1990?

5. What year did Bob Paisley retire?

6. Who replaced Bob Paisley as manager?

7. Who was the first signing of Kenny Dalglish's reign?

8. What did Joe Fagan win in his first season?

9. Who was appointed as Joe Fagan's replacement?

10.-In 1986 one player scored the most goals ever scored in a calendar year for Liverpool but who did it?

1981-1990

11. In 1989 Liverpool recorded their biggest first division win of 9-0 over Crystal palace, but how many goal scorers were there?

12. Who did the reds beat in the 1981 European cup final?

13. Who did Liverpool beat to secure the 1983 league title?

14. Who was Liverpool's kit manufacturer from 1985-1996?

15. Who scores the winning penalty to win the clubs forth European cup?

16. In 1982 who did Liverpool beat to win the league cup?

17. What was Joe Fagan's first trophy as manager?

18. What manager won Liverpool their first double/

19. Who holds the record for most goals scored at Anfield?

20. Who did Liverpool beat in the 1986 Fa Cup final?

1981-1990

21- Who scored the winning goal in the 1981 European cup final?

22-What was the score in the 1982 League cup final?

23- What was Kenny Dalglish's job title when appointed?

24-Who scored a brace in the 1986 Fa cup final?

25- Who did Liverpool beat in the 1982 Community Shield?

26-Draws against which two teams were enough to seal the clubs 15th title?

27-What was unique about the way Liverpool collected the 1983 league cup ?

28-What player appeared in "The Anfield Rap" a song marking Liverpools appearance in the 1988 FA Cup final?

29-In 1986 Liverpool took the league title from what reigning champions?

30-Who scored in the 1982 Community Shield?

1981-1990

31-Who was the manager for Liverpool's 15th league title?

32-What was unique about the 1984 League cup final?

33-Which player holds the record for most assists in a season for Liverpool with 24 in the 1984/85 season?

34- Who did Bob Paisley make captain in 1982?

35-How many minutes did it take Liverpool to score in the 1981 European cup final?

36-Who scored in the 1981 League cup final?

37-Who did Liverpool beat to win the 1989 Fa cup?

38-Who did Liverpool come from behind to beat and win their 18th title?

39-With a win in 1981 how many community Shields had Liverpool won in a row?

40-What was the score of the 1989 fa cup final?

1981-1990

41-Who did Liverpool share the 1990 Community Shield?

42-How many games did Liverpool win in their 1983 league title win?

43-Who did Liverpool beat in the 1988 Community Shield Final?

44-Liverpool beat Everton in the 1984 league cup final in a replay at what ground ?

45-Who scored to win the 18th League title?

46-What was the score when Liverpool beat Arsenal in the 1989 Community Shield?

47-Who did Liverpool beat in the 1983 league cup final?

48-Who scored the winning goal in the 1984 league cup final?

49-Who scored in the 1983 League cup final?

50-Where was the 1981 Champions league final played?

1991-2000

1. In 1993 which Liverpool player won PFA Young Player of the year?

2. In 2000 who made the European debut for Liverpool?

3.Who scored the first goal of the decade in 2000?

4.Who was the last signing of Kenny Dalglish's reign?

5. Who scored in Liverpool's fifth fa cup win?

6.Which second division team did Liverpool beat in the 1992 Fa Cup final?

7.Who replaced Kenny Dalglish as manager in 1991?

8.In 1992 Ian Rush becomes Liverpool's all time record goal scorer, taking over who?

9.Who did Ian Rush score against to become Liverpools all time record goal scorer?

10.What did Graeme Souness win as Liverpool manager?

1991-2000

11.In 1995 Liverpool beat who to lift their fifth league cup?

12-Who scored the last goal of the 1900's?

13-Who scored a brace to see Liverpool win the 1995 league cup?

14-With a team including Michael Owen and Jamie Carragher who do Liverpool beat to win the inaugural Fa Youth Cup?

15-Who won back to back PFA Young player of the year awards in 1995-1996?

16-In 1998 who joins Liverpool working as join manager alongside Roy Evans?

17-How long does the joint reign last before Roy Evans steps down?

18-Who is the clubs oldest debut goal scorer?

19-How many trophies did Kenny Dalglish win in his first reign as Liverpool manager?

20-In the 1991-1992 season who was Liverpools top goalscorer?

1991-2000

21- In 1992 who made their European debut to become Liverpools youngest ever player to play in Europe

22-In 1992 what Liverpool player becomes the top goalscorer in Fa Cup finals

23-Who was Kenny Dalglish's record signing

24-Who scored a 5 minute hat-trick against Arsenal

25- Who made the most appearances of the 1990-91 season

26-Who was Roy Evans last signing

27-Who replaced Graeme Souness in 1994

28-How many trophies did Roy Evans win

29-Who was Gerard Houllier's

30-During his short spell how many matches did Ronnie Moran take charge of

1991-2000

31-Who was Graeme Souness's record signing

32-How many managers did Liverpool have between 1991-2000

33-What country was Roy Evans the assistant manager of

34-Who was Gerard Houlliers first signing

35-How many games did Ian Rush play for his country

36-How many players did Roy Evans sign

37-Who was the sponsor for the league cup when Liverpool won it in 1995

38-How many games did Graeme Souness take charge of

39-What year did Ian Rush win the European Golden boot

40-Who was the top goalscorer in the 1991/92 season?

1991-2000

31-Who was Graeme Souness's record signing

32-How many managers did Liverpool have between 1991-2000

33-What country was Roy Evans the assistant manager of

34-Who was Gerard Houlliers first signing

35-How many games did Ian Rush play for his country

36-How many players did Roy Evans sign

37-Who was the sponsor for the league cup when Liverpool won it in 1995

38-How many games did Graeme Souness take charge of

39-What year did Ian Rush win the European Golden boot

40-Who was the top goalscorer in the 1991/92 season?

1991-2000

41-Who scored the most goals of Graeme Souness's reign?

42-How many games did Roy Evans manage a Liverpool manager?

43-Who did Ian Rush play his farewell game at Anfield against?

44-Who scored 5 goals in a league cup game against Fulham?

45-After scoring 5 goals against Luton what pre match ritual did Ian Rush continue for the rest of his career?

46-Who was Roy Evans record signing?

47-What country is Ian Rush from?

48 -How many teams did Graeme Souness manage?

49 How many managers did the reds have in the 1990's

50-Who did Ian Rush score his 300th goal against?

2001-2010

1. In the league cup in 2001 who became the oldest goal scorer in Liverpool's history?

2. Who was the only player to win PFA Player of the year for Liverpool between 2001-2010?

3.How many trophies did Liverpool win between 2001-2010?

4.Who was the first signing of Roy Hodson's reign?

5. Who was Liverpools iconic kit sponsor from 1996-2006?

6.Who did Liverpool play in their 5000th game?

7.Who did Liverpool beat on penalties in the 2001 league cup final?

8.Who did Liverpool beat for their fifth Champions league trophy?

9.Who scored twice in the 2001 Fa Cup final?

10.What was the score in the 2001 UEFA Cup final?

2001-2010

11. Who was the last signing of Roy Hodgson's reign?

12. Who did Liverpool beat in the 2001 Fa Cup Final?

13- What was notable about the trophy Liverpool were given for their fifth title ?

14- Who was the only Liverpool player to win the Football Writers footballer of the year between 2001-2010?

15- Who did Liverpool beat in August 2001 to win the Community Shield?

16- In 2006 who did the reds beat in the Fa Cup final ?

17- Who bought Liverpool in the 2006/07 season?

18- In October 2009 what objected assisted Darren Bent against Liverpool?

19- Who scored in the 2003 League cup final?

20- What was the 2006 FA cup final named by Liverpool fans?

2001-2010

21- How many times was Steven Gerrard in the PFA Team of the year between 2001-10?

22-Rafa Benitez became Liverpool manager after leaving which club?

23-Who did Liverpool beat at the Millennium stadium in August 2006 to win the Community Shield?

24- Which German giants did Liverpool beat to win the 2001/02 Super cup?

25- Where was the 2005/06 Super cup held?

26-Who sold Liverpool in 2007?

27-Who won the PFA fans player of the year twice between 2001-2010?

28-Liverpool broke their transfer record to sign who in 2007?

29-What was the fee?

30-Who scored the three goals to get Liverpool level in the 2005 Champions league final?

2001-2010

31-In 2010 who scored Liverpool's 9000th goal?

32- Who did Liverpool beat to win the 2005/06 Super cup?

33-Who was Rafa Benitez's record signing?

34-What manager won Liverpool's fifth Champions league?

35-Who was Rafa Benitez's record sale?

36-What country was Gerard Houllier from?

37.When Benitez left at the end of the 2009-10 season who was appointed as his successor?

38-Where was the 2003 League cup final help?

39-How many trophies did Liverpool win between 2001-10?

40-How many trophies did Gerard houllier win with Liverpool?

2001-2010

41-What English team did Liverpool beat in the semi-final on the way to their fifth Champions league?

42-Who did Steven Gerrard make his debut against?

43-Who captained the team for the 2005 Champions league final?

44-How many trophies did Rafa Benitez win with Liverpool?

45-Who did Gerard Houllier make his assistant manager?

46.In 2010 Who bought Liverpool FC?

47-Who did Liverpool play in the 2007 Champions league final?

48-What country is Rafa Benitez from?

49-How many games did Rafa Benitez manage?

50.Who did Roy Hodgson manage before Liverpool?

2011-2020

1. Liverpool won the Champions league in 18/19 taking their total to what?

2. How many Premier leagues do Liverpool have?

3.Between 2014-2018 how many players did Liverpool buy from Southampton?

4.-What red made one appearance during a loan at Real Madrid from Rio Ave?

5.What player played for Bayern Munich, inter Milan and Stoke before Liverpool?

6.Who wore Number 19 before moving to number 10 after Philippe Coutinho left the club?

7.Who was given vice captaincy and the number 7 in his first season?

8.What current Arsenal player trained with and almost signed for Liverpool in 2014?

9.In 2016/17 who became the first player to wear the number 66 for Liverpool?

10.In a league cup game in 2016 who became Liverpool's youngest goal scorer?

2011-2020

11. Between 2011-2020 how many Liverpool players won Premier league player of the season?

12. How many manager of the month awards did Liverpool win between 2011-2020 ?

13- In 2011 who became Liverpool manager for the second time?

14- Who was Liverpool's kit manufacturer from 2012-2015 ?

15- In 2020 what Liverpool player won PFA Young player of the year?

16- Who was the first signing of Jurgen Klopp's reign?

17- Who is the only Liverpool player to win the Best FIFA goalkeeper award?

18- In the 2018/19 Champions league winning season, who had the most assists?

19- In January 2018 Liverpool made their most expensive signing of all time, but who was it for?

20- Who did Salah make his debut against in 2017?

2011-2020

21- How many Premier league players of the month did Liverpool win between 2011-2020?

22-What was unique about the March 2014 player of the month award?

23-Who did Sadio Mane make his debut against in 2016?

24-In 2018 Liverpool sold a player for their biggest fee- who was it?

25- How many times did a Liverpool player win African footballer of the year between 2011-2020?

26-Who scored Liverpool's 10000th goal?

27-Who has scored the most Champions League penalties for Liverpool?

28-Who was the last Liverpool player to win Football writers footballer of the year?

29-Who did Van Dijk make his debut against in 2018?

30-In the 2019/20 Premier league winning season what player made the most appearances for the club?

2011-2020

31-In 2018 Liverpool signed their most expensive goalkeeper of all time but who was it?

32-Who was Liverpools kit manufacturer from 2015-17?

33-In 2018 Liverpool signed Alisson, but how much did they pay for him?

34-Between 2011-2020 how many Liverpool players have won PFA player of the year?

35-Steven Gerrard retired in 2015 but who did he score his last goal against?

36-What was the fastest goal Liverpool scored between 2010-2020?

37-What Liverpool player has the most England Caps?

38-In the 2015/16 season Liverpool saw the most different players score for them in one season but how many players scored?

39-Who did Liverpool beat to win their sixth Champions league trophy?

40-In 2017/18 who scored the most goals in a debut season of any Liverpool player in the clubs history?

2011-2020

41-In 2016 who scored in a 2-0 win over Leeds to become Liverpools all time youngest debut goalscorer?

42-Who did Trent Alexander-Arnold make his debut against in 2016?

43-Who do Liverpool beat on penalties to win the League cup in 2012?

44-Brendan Rodgers becomes the 19th manager of Liverpool after impressing at what club?

45-In 2019 a League cup game against Aston Villa saw the most debuts of any Liverpool match but how many players made their debut?

46-In 2016 what opens at Anfield?

47- In 2017 what did liverpool FC celebrate?

48.What was unique about the date of Liverpools first premier league title win?

49-In 2019 who did Liverpool beat in the semi final of the Club World Cup?

50-Who did Roberto Firmino make his debut against in 2015 ?

2020-

1. Who scored the winning penalty in the 21/22 league cup final?

2. Where do Liverpool's women's team play their home games?

3. Who scored a surprise 95th minute winner against West Brom in 2021?

4. The signing of Luis Diaz makes him the first Colombian player to play for Liverpool but he is not the first Columbian player to sign for Liverpool who is?

5. Why has the Columbian never played for Liverpool?

6. What current Liverpool has come of the bench in the premier league most of any Liverpool player?

7. Who became the Kit supplier for Liverpool in 2020?

8.-Who was the last player to score on their birthday?

9. In 2020 Liverpool bought Diogo Jota but who did he sign from?

10.-Which two current Liverpool players have the most goal/assist combinations?

2020-

11.Who has been Liverpool's shirt sponsor since 2010?

12-Who was the last player to score on their Anfield debut?

13-In Jan 2022-March 2022 Liverpool went on their all-time longest win streak, but how many games did they win?

14-Who scored the first goal of the new decade in 2020?

15-How many times has a Liverpool player scored more than 30 goals in a season?

16-Who became Liverpool women's manager for the second spell in 2021?

17-How many penalty shootouts have Liverpool won under Klopp?

18-Which two Liverpool players battled it out in the AFCON Final in 2021?

19-How many players have scored on their Anfield debut?

20- In 2021 Liverpool loaned the only Turkish player in their history but what was his name?

2020-

21- Who did Liverpool play in the 2022 League cup final?

22-How many South-American players have played for Liverpool?

23-How many matches were left when the reds won their first premier league title?

24-What is Liverpool's new training ground called?

25- What famous singer is a Liverpool fan and did a cover of "You'll never walk alone" ?

26-How many managers have Liverpool's women team had?

27-Who did Liverpool play in the League cup Semi-final?

28-What was Liverpool's old training ground called?

29-How man trophies has Klopp Won?

30-Who was bought from Preston during the 20/21 season?

2020-

31-Two players made 51 appearances during the 20/21 season, who were they?

32-How many points did the title winners amas?

33-Who debuted against Chelsea in September 2020?

34-What famous Merseyside actor and Liverpool fan can be found as the voice over on the Anfield tour?

35-Who is Liverpool's penalty taker?

36-Who did liverpool buy from German side RB Leipzig in 2021?

37-Who was added to the sleeve sponsor in 2020?

38-Who won Liverpool goal of the season 2020/21?

39-Who was the highest goalscorer in the 20/21 season?

40-Who is Jurgen Klopp's assistant?

2020-

41-Who won Liverpool women fans player of the year in 2020/21?

42-How many wins did the title winning reds make in the league?

43-Who won Liverpool mens player of the year in 2020/21?

44-Which Liverpool player scored the winning penalty in the AFCON final?

45-Which German player was loaned out to Bundesliga side Union Berlin in 2021?

46-How many penalty shootouts were Liverpool involved in during the 2021/22 League cup?

47-Which ex academy and now first team player has a mural outside Anfield?

48-Who won Liverpool men fans player of the year 2019/20?

49-What NBA Player owns a part of Liverpool?

50-What other Premier league club did Mo Salah play for?

ANSWERS-MANAGERS

1. 2012-2015
2. Two
3. Two
4. William Edward Barclay
5. Fourteen
6. 1882-96
7. Dortmund and Mainz
8. Relegation
9. Norbert
10. Fa Cup, League Cup, Europa league
11. Newcastle,Chelsea,Everton
12. Scotland
13- Rafeal Benitez
14- Eight
15- Heavy Metal
16- Bob Paisley
17- Jurgen Klopp
18- Bob Paisley
19- Mainz
20- Bill Shankly
21- Ballymena United
22- Twelve
23- Brendan Rodgers
24- Carlisle United
25- Four

ANSWERS-MANAGERS

26. Jurgen Klopp.
27. Kenny Dalglish.
28. Bob Paisley.
29. Touch the "This is Anfield sign".
30. His glasses.
31. Adam Lallana.
32. Bill Shankly.
33. Bob Paisley.
34. Don Welsh.
35. Mainz.
36. Brendan Rodgers.
37. Tom Watson.
38. Rafael Benetiz.
39. 2019.
40. Tom Watson.
41. Sir Kenny Dalglish.
42. Jurgen Klopp.
43. Bill Shankly.
44. Seven.
45. Bob Paisley.
46. Sir Kenny Dalglish.
47. Sir Kenny Dalglish.
48. Zeljko Buvac.
49. Joe Fagan.
50. Graeme Souness.

ANSWERS-PLAYERS

1.Ian Rush.

2. Ian Callaghan.

3.Robbie Fowler and Sadio Mane.

4.He was setting up an ironing board.

5. Chelsea-Kepa.

6.Mohamed Salah Ghaly.

7.Alisson.

8.Van Dijk.

9.Mane and Salah.

10.Ballotelli.

11.Rickie Lambert.

12.Bruce Grobbelaar.

13.Ian Rush.

14.Steve Heighway.

15.John Wark.

16.Jack Balmer.

17.Rush.

18.One.

19.Three.

20.Salah.

21.Antonio nunez.

22.Joe Cole 27 seconds.

23.Daniel Sturridge.

24.Fifteen.

25.3 Mane,Origi,Salah.

ANSWERS-PLAYERS

26.Pepe Reina.

27.Firmino.

28.Jota.

29.Firminio.

30. Fabinho.

31.Thiago.

32.Nineteen.

33.He scored his thirteenth hattrick for the club.

34.Ian Rush.

35.Steven Gerrard.

36.Mo Salah.

37.Sadio Mane.

38.Wijnaldum.

39.Salah.

40.Dejan Lovren.

41.Aston Villa.

42.4 Salah,Mane, Van Dijk, Henderson.

43.Elisha scott , 21 years 52 days.

44.Steven Gerrard.

45.Ray Clemence.

46.Jerome Sinclair 16 years 6 days.

47.Sadio Mane.

48.Jamie Carragher 264.

49.Steven Gerrard.

50.Bruce Grobbelaar.

51.(14)

ANSWERS-CAPTAINS

1. Jordan Henderson.
2. Steven Gerrard.
3. 10 James Milner (24), Jordan Henderson (23), Lucas Leiva (8), Kolo Touré (2), Joe Allen (1), Christian Benteke (1), Jose Enrique (1), Jon Flanagan (1), Mamadou Sakho (1), Martin Skrtel (1).
4. 4 Henderson, Milner, Van Dijk Winjaldum.
5. Jordan Henderson.
6. What season was Steven Gerrard made captain (2003/04)
7. 20.
8. Two.
9. Willem II.
10. Swansea-League cup 2014.
11. Partick Thistle.
12. Steven Gerrard 472.
13. 312.
14. 86 goals.
15. Spurs.
16. 2.
17. 10 years.
18. 11.
19. Steven Gerrard.
20. He was immediately appointed.
2. Steven Gerrard 472.
22. £65,000.
23. Andrew Hannah.
24. 23
25. Ron Yeats.

ANSWERS-CAPTAINS

26.Celtic 6-0 December 1994.

27.Steven Gerrard 12 years.

28.Bill Shankly took the captaincy from Tommy Smith after complaining about being left out of a game.

29.Olympiacos, 2-0 August 2013.

30.Sunderland.

3.It was his final game for the club.

32.5.

33.1971.

34.Sami Hyypia.

35.148.

36.England XL 2-0 1988.

37.Three.

38.Blackpool.

39.16.2m.

40.2.

41.8.

42.4 years.

43.Southampton League cup 2002.

44.Emlyn Hughes.

45.New Brighton Tower 2-0 September 1899.

46.5.

47.Being a TV Pundit.

48.Gerard Houllier.

49.Phil Thompson.

50.Borussia Monchengladbach 0-1 March 1979.

ANSWERS-ANFIELD

1.53,394.

2. 1884

3.61,905 vs Wolves in 1952

4.The Kop, The Main Stand, The Anfield Road stand, The Sir Kenny Dalglish Stand.

5.False it's the 7th after, Wembley, Old Trafford, Tottenham Hotspur stadium, Emirates, London Stadium and Etihad.

6.Everton.

7.Lincoln.

8.5000.

9.1982.

10.68 games from April 2017-Jan 2021.

11.Goodison Park-Everton.

12.Bill Shankly.

13.You'll never walk alon..

14.Van Dijk.

15.Bill Shankly, Bob Paisley.

16.The Anfield Road stand.

17.61,000.

18.Everton vs Earlstown 28th September 1884.

19.1957.

20.4th December 1997.

21.30th January 2020.

22.Kopites.

23.Main Stand.

24.Champions league/European cup.

25.George Gillett and Tom Hicks.

ANSWERS-ANFIELD

26. England vs Ireland 1889.

27. November 2019 vs Everton.

28. 5.

29. 1929.

30. 2006- England 2-1 win over Uruguay.

31. Manchester United, 3-1 win over Arsenal.

32. Take that, Bon Jovi and pink.

33. Elton John and The Eagles.

34. Archibald Leitch.

35. 29,000.

36. 20,676.

37. FSG.

38. five.

39. Shankly's widow Nessie.

40. Journalist Ernest Edwards.

41. It was the topmast of the SS Great Eastern, one of the first iron ships.

42. 9074.

43. 1906.

44. He was an evangelical preacher.

45. 2016-17.

46. 24.

47. 12,850.

48. 85.

49. Kirkdale Stadium.

50. 11,762.

ANSWERS-FAMOUS GAMES

1.Penalties.

2. Arsenal.

3.West Ham.

4.10.

5.It was the first time the club had ever played in June.

6.True, Glasgow, Cardiff, London.

7.Two.

8.Matip.

9.Atletico Madrid's ground Wanda Metropolitano.

10.Dejan Lovren.

11.Divock Origi.

12.Twice.

13.Roma.

14.79 points.

15.It was two legs.

16.Peter Crouch.

17.Scotland.

18.7.

19.The first team were playing in the club world cup.

20.10-0 in 1986/87 vs Fulham FC.

21.Cardiff City.

22.Minamino.

23.Four.

24.Flamengo.

25.10-1 Oulun Palloseura.

ANSWERS-FAMOUS GAMES

26. 14 seconds.

27. Chelsea.

28. Dominic Solanke.

29. Alan Kennedy.

30. Millennium stadium-Cardiff.

31. It was closed for reconstruction.

32. 9.

33. Mo Salah.

34. Penalties.

35. Gordon Hodgson 17.

36. Michael Owen.

37. 15.

38. 9:0 vs Crystal palace.

39. They were the first English team to win every game of the Champions' league group stage.

40. An extra time own goal.

41. Leeds.

42. 463.

43. Mo Salah.

44. Third.

45. They're shared.

46. West Ham.

47. Ned Doig 37 years 10 months 3 days-1904.

48. Jamie Carragher.

49. Middlesbrough 2006.

50. Kenny Dalglish 1984-85, 24.

ANSWERS-RIVALRIES

1.Everton.

2. Manchester United.

3.Mo Salah.

4.Michael Owen.

5.Matt Busby.

6.Peter Beardsley.

7.Gary Ablett.

8.Abel Xavier.

9.Everton

10.Jamie Carragher and Gary Neville.

11.Van Dijk.

13.Karius.

14.Liverpool.

15. It's produced the most red cards of any fixture.

16.The North West Derby.

17.Everton.

18.17.

19.Ray Clemence 15 clean sheets in 27 games.

20.239.

21.20.

22.Divock Origi.

23.Tranmere Rovers.

24.Ian Rush.

25.25.

ANSWERS-RIVALRIES

26.3 games between 2011-2020.

27.9).

28.78,299 at Goodison Park September 1984.

29.4.

30.47.

31.208.

32.6-0 in 1935.

34.Gerrard.

36.2.

37.15.

38-Ian Rush 36 games.

39.5.

40.6.

41.4 drew 2.

42.4.

43.1 Tie, 2 games.

44.Jamie Carragher.

45.Newton Heath.

46.Because Old Trafford was closed due to war damage- they had been playing at Manchester City ground Maine Road but City had a home game against Chelsea that day so it was moved to Goodison.

47.38.

48.Planned for 5 times but one game was cancelled in 2020, so four.

49.Once 2011-12.

50.Wayne Rooney.

1.Blue and white.

2. Malcolm Mcvean.

3.John Houlding.

4.Everton Athletic.

5.(7-1)

6.They were all Scottish.

7.The Lancashire League.

8.Tom Watson.

9.Newcastle.

10.Jock Smith.

11.Grimsby Town.

12.3rd June.

14.Sunderland.

14.Middlesbrough.

15.March 15th 1892.

16.8-0.

17.Higher Walton.

18.Because the FA didn't accept two clubs being called Everton.

19.10-1.

20.William Edward Barclay.

21.Jimmy Scott.

22.John McKenna.

23.Dublin.

24.1896.

25.Two).

26.3.

27.John Mckenna.

28.Everton.

29.1857.

30.Archie Goldie.

31.Blackpool.

32.1.

33.3-1.

34.It was the first match Liverpool played in red.

35.John Miller.

36.25.

37.36.

38.Northwich Victoria.

39.One.

40.Ireland.

41.Harry Bradshaw.

42.16.

43.They doubled his wage to £300 a year.

44.Duncan McLean and Matt McQueen.

45.Willie Michael.

46.Johnny Walker.

47.Scotland.

48-Aston Villa.

49.Robert Neill.

50.3-3.

ANSWERS-1901-1910

1. Sam Raybould.
2. Sam Raybould.
3. Sam Raybould.
4. New Brighton Tower.
5. Once.
6. Hurlford Scotland.
7. Stoke.
8. 742.
9. Bobby Robinson.
10. £500.
11. 2-1900/01,1905/06.
12. Hibernian.
13. 1904/05.
14. Newcastle United.
15. George Livingstone.
16. 363.
17. 8.
18. Blackpool.
19. 1.
20. £460.
21. 271.
22. 678.
23. 361.
24. 3.
25. 31.

26.8.

27.Chesterfield Town.

28.Middlesbrough.

29.130.

30-.Alex Raisbeck.

31.80.

32.24.

33.Arthur Goddard.

34.414.

35.Sunderland.

36.56.

37.Burton United.

38.361.

39.1.

40.Doncaster Rovers.

41.1905/06.

42.Sam Raybould.

43.£340.

44.Nottingham Forest.

45.Aston Villa.

46.6.

47.£250.

48.14.

49.221.

50.Bury.

ANSWERS-1911-1920

1. Burnley.
2. Preston North End.
3. The Wednesday.
4. Ephraim Longworth.
5. Alf West.
6. Ephraim Longworth.
7. Thirty nine
8. George Patterson.
9. Tottenham Hotspur.
10. 141.
11. 370.
12. Fred Pagnam.
13. It was asking for players to sign for Liverpool.
14. Newcastle United.
15. Nineteen
16. Bolton Wanders.
17. He was given a testimonial after only two years at the club.
18. Fred Pagman.
19. Blackpool.
20. 13.05.1912.
21. He had an outstanding goal to game ratio 30 goals in 39 games.
22. Sunderland.
23. Third Lanark.
24. 434.
25. John Miller.

26.Arthur goddard.

27.Jimmy Nicholl.

28.Manager Tom Watson.

29.3.

30.Ephraim Longworth.

31.Arthur Goddard.

32.Jack Parkinson.

33.Newcastle United.

34.18 years.

35.14.

36.125.

37.Tom Bennett.

38.4.

39.Newton Villa.

40.Luton Town.

41.Bob Ferguson.

42.Jack Parkinson.

43.Blackburn Rovers.

44.29.

45.Jock McNab.

46.37.

47.37.

48.121.

49.Bolton Wanderers.

50.Bradford.

1. Oldham Athletic.
2. 1922/23 1923/24.
3. A roof was added to the kop.
4. George Patterson.
5. Cyril Oxley.
6. Donald McKinlay-194.
7. Raising Liverpool's prestige.
8. Bill Cockburn.
9. 366.
10. Birmingham.
11. He was a director at the club.
12. 242.
13. Dick Forshaw.
14. Jack Sambrook.
15. 17.
16. Dick Forshaw-74.
17. Walter Wadsworth.
18. 1863.
19. True.
20. 2.
21. 366.
22. Scotland.
23. He joined the coaching staff.
24. Kenny Dalglish.
25. Manchester United.

26 .339.
27.Bristol City.
28.Belfast, Ireland.
29.229.
30.Middlesbrough.
31.31.
32.151.
33.The Wednesday.
34.24.
35.Jimmy Walsh.
36.224.
37.15.
38.1.
39.Sheffield United.
40.22.
41.Aberdeen.
42.375.
43.Stockport County.
44.Sunderland.
45.11.
46.He became a minister.
47.25.
48.£1750.
49.Sunderland.
50.22.

ANSWERS-1931-1940

1. 354.
2. Albert Stubbins.
3. Jack Balmer-282.
4. Tottenham Hotspur
5. 122.
6. Everton.
7. Gordon Hodgson
8. (27).
9. Arsenal.
10. Alf Hobson
11. Jack Balmer
12. 107.
13. Matt Busby.
14. 377,
15. 37.
16. Liverpool, England.
17. 29/08/1936.
18. Stan Palk.
19. Matthew Fitzsimmons.
20. 321.
21. Derby.
22. 8.
23. 58 players.
24. Albert Stubbins.
25. Newcastle United.

26. Southampton.

27.4.

28.Luton town and Southampton.

29.Grimsby Town.

30.1.

31.Bristol Rovers.

32.£8000.

33.160.

34.Manchester.

35.15.

36.Scotland.

37.Bristol.

38.Lancashire FC.

39. Manchester United.

40.First Division.

4.36.

42.291.

43.Derby County.

44.Wolves and Arsenal.

45.10.

46.Transvaal.

47.168.

48.Passing.

49.He was giant.

50.241.

1.Albert Stubbins.
2.Phil Taylor.
3.Jack Balmer.
4. Portsmouth, Derby County, Arsenal.
5.3.
6.He became chief coach for the club before becoming manager.
7.Tranmere rovers.
8.1.
9.277.
10.Southampton.
11.60.
12.Chester.
1.54.
14.Sunderland.
15. 5.
16.13.
17.Manchester United.
18.Phil Taylor.
19.£4000.
20.Don Woan.
21.257.
22.326.
23.Charlton.
24.1950.
25.Arsenal.

26.122.

27.Bishop Auckland.

28.Middlesbrough.

29.Sunderland.

30.Seven,

31.342.

32.South Africa.

33.One

34.A physiotherapist and masseur.

35.Jimmy Payne.

36.Cyril Done.

37.Bolton Wanderers.

38.Nine.

39.The Fa Cup.

40.Sunderland.

41.2.

42.Bolton Wanderers.

43.Bolton Wanderers.

44.Charlton Athletic, Grimsby Town.

45.Blackburn Rovers.

46.Huddersfield town, Charlton Athletic, Preston North End,Sunderland,Arsenal.

47.5.

48.243.

49.Chelsea.

50..Manchester United.

ANSWERS-1951-1960

1. 1959.
2. 24.
3. A boot storage room.
4. Arsenal
5. Bill Shankly.
6. Liverpool.
7. Billy Liddell.
8. Birmingham City.
9. Direct free kick.
10. Huddersfield Town.
11. Edinburgh, Scotland.
12. Phil Taylor.
13. Preston North end.
14. 36.
15. Hibernian.
16. 379.
17. They all played football.
18. Sales representative.
19. "The art of tackling.
20. The postman.
21. 61,905.
22. Manchester.
23. Ronnie Moran.
24. Sammy Reid.
25. 23.

26.Desmond Palmer.

27.Robbie Fowler.

28.£1500 a year, with an additional £500 for expenses.

29.Derby.

30.Chester.

31.1956.

32.Yes he played one game during WW2.

33.218.

34.Blackburn.

35.Bury.

36.Bristol.

37.Bristol City.

38.17.

39.27.

40.Charlton Athletic.

41.Brighton and Hove Albion, Bournemouth, Wycombe Wanderers.

42.Boxing.

43.17.

44.He became a publican.

45.He's the only Liverpool manager not to manage in the first division.

46.Grimsby.

47.9.

48.Preston North End.

49.Brighton and Hove Albion.

50.Southend.

ANSWERS-1961-1970

1. 1964.
2. The Fa Cup.
3. You'll never walk alone.
4. Phil Chisnall.
5. Ian St John.
6. Ray Clemence 323.
7. Ian St john.
8. £37,500.
9. Ron Yeats.
10. They were both Scottish.
11. That he would take Liverpool back to the top flight.
12. Five.
13. Southampton.
14. He sent the team out in an all red team.
15. European competition.
16. Reykjavik.
17. 6.
18. 11-1.
19. The stadium was already full.
20. Leeds.
21. Roger Hunt and Ian St John.
22. West Ham.
23. He sent out Gerry Byrne and Gordon Milne to parade the Fa Cup.
24. Manchester United.
25. Roger Hunt.

26.Everton.

27.Ian Callaghan.

28.Ray Clemence.

29.Ian Callahan.

30.Manchester United.

31.4.

32 .Motherwell.

33.Arsenal.

34.Roger Hunt.

35.857.

36.15.

37.Central midfield.

38.3.

39.Borussia Dortmund.

40.75 years.

41.It was the first time the club outright won it-
not sharing with another club.

42.43 years.

43-.Bill Shankly.

44.68.

45.13/01/1962.

46.609.

47.Nottingham forest.

48.6-1.

49.249.

50.Peter Wall.

1. Ian Rush.
2. Phil Neal.
3. The league title and UEFA Cup.
4. Bill Paisley.
5. League title and UEFA Cup.
6. The European Cup.
7. The Fa Cup.
8. League Cup.
9. Umbro.
10. Kenny Dalglish.
11. 9.
12. Thousands of Liverpool fans lined the streets to cheer and welcome the team back.
13. David Fairclough.
14. Leeds and Arsenal.
15. Borussia Monchengladbach.
16. Hitachi.
17. 3-0.
18. Newcastle United.
19. 3-0.
20. Terry McDermott.
21. West Ham.
22-. Aston Villa.
23. 1974.
24. Kenny Dalglish and Terry Mcdermott-2.
25. Kevin Keegan, Ray Kennedy, John Toshack.

26.6-0.

27.QPR.

28.0-0.

29.Rome.

30.Bill Shankly.

31.David Fairclough.

32.FC Bruges.

33.Glasgow.

34.4-3.

35.Wembley.

36.In a press conference at Anfield.

37.Penalties.

38.783.

39.10.

40.1919.

41.Leeds.

42.Bill Shankly

43.1913.

44.John Toshack.

45.Fc Bruges.

46.Kenny Dalglish.

47.68.

48.18.

49.Terry McDermott,Tommy Smith,Phil Neal.

50.Celtic.

1. Luton Town.

2. Newton Ladies FC.

3.Twice.

4.1983 Kenny Dalglish, 1984 Ian Rush, 1988 John Barnes, 1989 Steve Nicol.

5.1983.

6.Joe Fagan.

7.Steven McMahon.

8.The league, League cup and European cup.

9.Kenny Dalglish.

10.Ian Rush.

11.8.

12.Real Madrid.

13.Watford.

14.Adidas.

15.Alan Kennedy.

16.Tottenham Hotspur.

17.League cup.

18.Kenny Dalglish.

19.Ian Rush.

20.Everton.

21.Alan Kennedy.

22.3-1.

23.Player-manager.

24.Ian Rush.

25.Tottenham Hotspur.

26.Notts County and Norwich.

27.Captain Graeme Souness let Bob Paisley collect the trophy as he was leaving.

28.John Barnes.

29.Everton.

30.Ian Rush.

31.Joe Fagan.

32.It was the first ever Merseyside derby final.

33.Kenny Dalglish.

34.Graeme Souness.

35.81.

36.Alan Hansen and Kenny Dalglish.

37.Everton.

38.QPR 2-1.

39.5.

40.3-2.

41-Who did Liverpool share the 1990 Community Shield.

42.19.

43.Wimbledon.

44.Manchester City's Maine Road.

45.Ian Rush and John Barnes.

46.1-0.

47.Manchester United.

48.Graeme Souness.

49.Alan Kennedy and Ronnie Whelan.

50.(Paris)

1. Ian Rush.

2. Gary McAllister.

3. Patrik Berger.

4. David Speedie

5. Ian Rush and Michael Thomas.

6. Sunderland.

7. Graeme Souness.

8. Roger Hunt.

9. Manchester United.

10. The Fa Cup.

11. Bolton Wanderers.

12. Robbie Fowler.

13. Steve McManaman.

14. West Ham United.

15. Robbie Fowler.

16. Gerard Houllier.

17. 4 months.

18. Gary McAllister.

19. 11.

20. Dean Saunders.

21. Phil Charnock.

22. Ian Rush.

23. Ian Rush £2.8m.

24. Robbie Fowler.

25. Ian Rush.

26.Vegard Heggem.

27.Roy Evans.

28.1.

29.Emile Heskey.

30.9.

31.Dean Saunders.

32.5.

33.Wales.

34.Jean Michel Ferri.

35.73.

36.20.

37.Coca cola.

38.157.

39.1984.

40.Dean Saunders.

41.Ian Rush.

42.226.

43.Middlesbrough.

44.Robbie Fowler.

45.He wet his boots prior to kick off.

46. Stan Collymore.

47.Wales.

48.8.

49.3.

50.Tottenham.

ANSWERS-2001-2010

1. Gary McAllister.
2. Steven Gerrard.
3. 8.
4. Joe Cole.
5. Carlsberg.
6. Middlesbrough.
7. Birmingham city
8. AC Milan.
9. Michael Owen.
10. 5-4.
11. Suso.
12. Arsenal.
13. It was the last 'real' Champions league trophy given to the winning team.
14. Steven Gerrard.
15. Manchester United.
16. West Ham.
17. George Gillett and Tom Hicks.
18. A beach ball.
19. Steven Gerrard and Michael Owen.
20. The Gerrard final.
21. 7-2001/04/05/06/07/08/09.
22. Valencia.
23. Chelsea.
24. Bayern Munich.
25. Monaco.

26.David Moores.

27.Steven Gerrard 2001/09.

28.Fernando Torres.

29.£34m.

30.Steven Gerrard, Vladmir Smicer and Xabi Alonso.

31.Sotirios Kyrgiakos.

32.CSKA Moscow.

33.Fernando Torres.

34.Rafael Benitez.

35.Xabi Alonso £30m.

36.France.

37.Roy Hodgson.

38.Cardiff.

39.9.

4.4.

41.Chelsea.

42.Blackburn Rovers

43.Steven Gerrard.

44.3

45.Phil Thompson.

46.John Henry and Fenway Sports Group.

47. Ac Milan.

48.Spain.

49.350.

50.Fulham.

1.Six.

2.One.

3. Six.

4 Fabinho.

5.Shaqiri.

6. Sadio Mane.

7.James Milner .

8.Martin Odegaard.

9.Trent Alexander-Arnold.

10.Ben Woodburn.

11.3 Suarez, Salah,Van Dijk.

12.10-Brendan Rodgers 2 , Jurgen Klopp 8.

13.Kenny Dalglish.

14.Warrior Sport.

15.Trent Alexander-Arnold.

16.Marko Grujic.

17.Alisson Becker 2019.

18.Trent Alexander-Arnold 16.

19.Virgil Van Dijk.

20.Watford.

21.12.

22.2 players won it Suarez and Gerrard shared.

23.Sadio Mane.

24.Philippe Coutinho.

25.3 2017/18 Salah, 2019 Sadio Mane.

ANSWERS-2011-2020

26-.Diogo Jota.
27.Steven Gerrard 7.
28.Jordan Henderson-2020.
29.Virgil Van Dijk.
30.Roberto Firmino 52.
31.Alisson Becker-£65mil.
32.New Balance.
33.£65m.
34.Three 2014 Luis Suarez,2018 Mohamed Salah, 2019
Virgil Van Dijk.
35.Stoke City.
36.15 Seconds,Naby Keita vs Huddersfield town.
37.Steven Gerrard.
38.22.
39.Tottenham Hotspur.
40.Mo Salah 44.
41.Ben Woodburn
42-Spurs.
43.Cardiff City.
44.Swansea City.
45.8.
46.The new Main stand.
47.It's 125 birthday.
48.It was the earliest and latest a team had ever won
the league – earliest in game week but latest in date
due to postponement as a result of the COVID-19
pandemic.
49.Monterrey
50.Stoke City.

ANSWERS -2020-

1. Kelleher.
2. Prenton Park.
3. Alisson Becker.
4. Anderson Arroyo.
5 He hasn't managed to be granted a work permit.
6. Divock Origi 71.
7. Nike.
8. Takumi Minamino 2022
9. Wolves.
10. Firmino and Salah.
11. Standard Charter.
12. Kaide Gordon 2022.
13. 12.
14. Mo Salah.
15. 27 times.
16. Matt Beard.
17. 6- out of 10.
18. Salah and Mane.
19. 105.
20. Ozan Kabak.
21. Chelsea.
22. 17.
23. 7.
24. AXA Training centre.
25. Lana Del Rey.

ANSWERS -2020-

26.15.

27.Arsenal.

28.Melwood.

29.Five.

30.Ben Davies.

31.Georginio Wijnaldum and Mohamed Salah.

32.99.

33.Thiago.

34.David Morrissey.

35.Salah.

36.Ibrahima Konate.

37.Expedia.

38.Alisson vs West Brom.

39.Mo Salah.

40.Pepijn Lijnders.

41.Missy Bo Kearns.

42.32.

43.Mo Salah.

44.Sadio Mane.

45.Loris Karius.

46.2.

47.Trent Alexander Arnold.

48.Jordan Henderson.

49.Lebron James.

50.Chelsea.

WITH THANKS

KickNetGoalBooks thanks the following websites for their facts and knowledge of LFC for this book

LFCHistory.net
Wikipedia
LiverpoolFC.com

Thankyou for reading this book

Please leave a review on Amazon and check out our other books.

Printed in Great Britain
by Amazon

13496139R00088